A Primary Source History of

THE DUST BOWL

by Rebecca Langston-George

Consultant: David Wishart
Historical Geographer
School of Natural Resources
University of Nebraska-Lincoln

CAPSTONE PRESS
a capstone imprint

Fact Finders Books are published by Capstone Press,
1710 Roe Crest Drive, North Mankato, Minnesota 56003
www.capstonepub.com

Library of Congress Cataloging-in-Publication Data
Langston-George, Rebecca.
A primary source history of the Dust Bowl / by Rebecca Langston-George.
pages cm. — (Fact finders. Primary source history.)
Includes bibliographical references and index.
Summary: "Uses primary sources to tell the story of the Dust Bowl"— Provided by publisher.
ISBN 978-1-4914-1840-6 (library binding) — ISBN 978-1-4914-1844-4 (pbk.) — ISBN 978-1-4914-1848-2
(ebook pdf)
1. Dust Bowl Era, 1931-1939—Sources—Juvenile literature. 2. Depressions—1929—Great Plains—
Juvenile literature. 3. Great Plains—History—20th century—Juvenile literature. 4. Great Plains—Social
conditions—20th century—Juvenile literature. 5. Droughts—Great Plains—History—20th century—
Juvenile literature. 6. Farmers—Great Plains—Social conditions—20th century—Juvenile literature. I.
Title.
F595.L358 2015
973.917—dc23   2014014792

Editorial Credits
Jennifer Besel, editor; Kyle Grenz, designer; Wanda Winch, media researcher;
    Kathy McColley, production specialist

Photo Credits
Capstone, 6; Franklin D. Roosevelt Library, 29; kansasmemory.org, Kansas State Historical Society,
5, 14; Library of Congress: Prints and Photographs Division, cover (top), 1 (all), 8, 9, 11, 12, 17, 18,
19, 20, 21, 22, 23, 25, 27; National Archives and Records Administration (NARA), 10; Newscom:
Everett Collection, 13; National Oceanic and Atmospheric Administration (NOAA): NWS Collection/
George E. Marsh Album, cover (bottom); Panhandle Plains Historical Museum, Canyon, Texas, 15;
Shutterstock: natu, 22 (cotton); Trove: The Advertiser (Adelaide, SA), 16; United States Department of
Agriculture (USDA): B.C. McLean, 7, NRCS, 28

Printed in Canada.
092014   008478FRS15

TABLE OF CONTENTS

A NOTE ABOUT PRIMARY SOURCES

Primary sources are newspaper articles, photographs, speeches, or other documents that were created during an event. They are great ways to see how people spoke and felt during that time. You'll find primary sources from the time of the Dust Bowl throughout this book. Within the text, primary source quotations are colored **red** and set in italic type.

THE BLACK BLIZZARD

"Black and saffron clouds of dust—spectacular, menacing, intensely irritating to man and beast alike, choking, blowing out tender crops, and lasting without mercy for days—have darkened everything ..."
—from "If It Rains" by reporter Robert Geiger

Those fierce black clouds were part of a dust storm that blew across the **Great Plains** at more than 50 miles (80 kilometers) per hour from Kansas to Texas. The Black Blizzard blotted out the sun and plunged day into night. Flocks of birds raced to outrun the storm. Gritty sand blasted paint from houses and cars. People ran for cover, shuttering windows and doors.

But nothing could keep the dust from blowing in. It blew through cracks, covering tables, beds, and dinner plates with fine dust. Dirt piles several feet high pressed against buildings. Crops were destroyed. Livestock choked to death.

Great Plains—the broad, level land that stretches eastward from the base of the Rocky Mountains for about 400 miles (644 km) in the United States and Canada

△ Dust storms, like the Black Blizzard on April 14, blew away about 850 million tons (771 million metric tons) of top soil in 1935.

The Black Blizzard of April 14, 1935, was one of the worst dust storms in American history. But it was only one of hundreds of severe "dusters" to hit the plains states during the 1930s. These storms earned the area the nickname the Dust Bowl.

THE DUST BOWL

Drought affected 50 million acres (20 million hectares) of the Great Plains. But the worst conditions were found around the Oklahoma and Texas **panhandles**, and this area became known as the Dust Bowl.

DROUGHT IN THE PLAINS

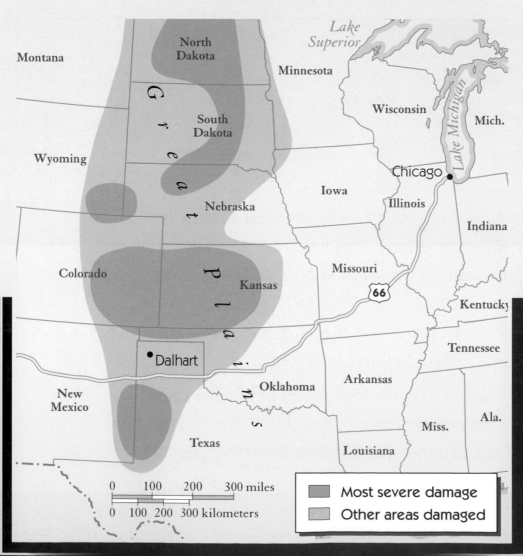

	Most severe damage
	Other areas damaged

Severe drought, plowing, and soil **erosion** created the Dust Bowl conditions. The flat, treeless plains that were once sheltered with a carpet of short grasses became parched and covered in sand drifts. From 1930 to about 1940, much of the Dust Bowl looked like a desert. But it wasn't until the Black Blizzard of 1935 that the area gained its famous Dust Bowl name. Robert Geiger, an Associated Press reporter, wrote *"Three little words ... rule life in the dust bowl ... if it rains."*

panhandle—a narrow area of land that sticks out from a larger land area
erosion—the wearing away of land by water or wind

7

DROUGHT

The crops, livestock, and people of the Great Plains depended upon rain for survival. Rain watered the crops. It filled drinking wells. But for 10 years during the 1930s, little rain fell. Churches even began holding services to pray for rain.

Hoping and praying for rain proved unsuccessful. Scientists studying the situation wrote, *"... crop cultivation over the greater part of this territory is ... doomed to failure."*

Without rain farmers' crops died. Fruits and vegetables in family gardens died. Soon the livestock that families depended upon for meat and money died too. Problem after problem could be traced back to drought.

▷ Blowing topsoil covered animals' watering holes, making survival very difficult.

Titled "Going to church to pray for rain," this image was taken in July 1936 by Arthur Rothstein. Rothstein's image of life in North Dakota shows how desperate people in the Midwest were for rain. ▷

Rainfall in the Oklahoma Panhandle 1931–1940

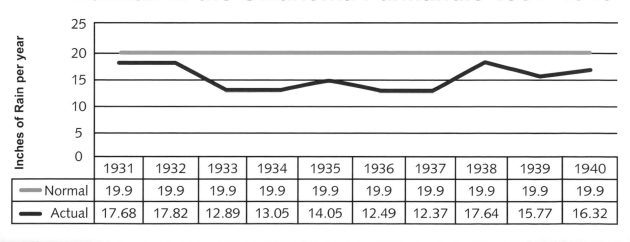

	1931	1932	1933	1934	1935	1936	1937	1938	1939	1940
Normal	19.9	19.9	19.9	19.9	19.9	19.9	19.9	19.9	19.9	19.9
Actual	17.68	17.82	12.89	13.05	14.05	12.49	12.37	17.64	15.77	16.32

PLOWS AND WIND

Soil erosion also contributed to the Dust Bowl. Before settlers moved in, the Great Plains were covered by thick grasses. But as more people moved into the plains, they began to change the natural landscape. In 1862 Congress passed the Homestead Act, which promised each settler 160 acres (65 hectares) of land. Thousands of people moved for the chance to own land. Then in 1907 lawmakers admitted the new state of Oklahoma. Once again the government lured settlers with offers of cheap land. Thousands more people rushed to what was once called Indian Territory.

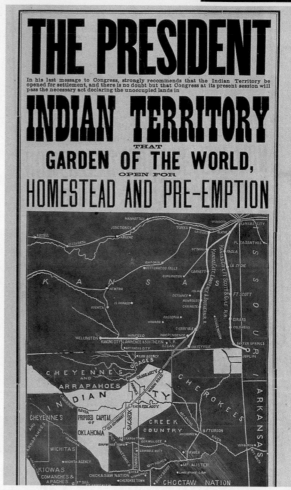

△ Posters advertising the fertile land in Indian Territory encouraged settlers to farm the land.

Homesteaders had to promise to improve the land. So they dug up the prairie grasses and planted wheat. At first the wheat was successful. But in those early days, the weather was unusually rainy. Soon the drought came, and the wheat died. The native grasses were gone, so nothing held the soil in place. Loose, parched dirt easily scattered with the wind.

Farmers had also been plowing and planting for years without giving the soil a chance to recover. The soil lost its **nutrients** and became unproductive. President Franklin D. Roosevelt wrote, *"The basic cause of the present Great Plains situation is an attempt to impose upon the region a system of agriculture to which the Plains are not adapted—to bring into a semi-arid region methods which are suitable, on the whole, only for a humid region."*

CRITICAL THINKING

President Roosevelt stated the Great Plains were not adapted to the methods of agriculture being used. Yet the advertisement called the territory "that garden of the world." How might merchants and land developers have benefited by calling the area a garden?

nutrient—a substance needed by a living thing to stay healthy

Farmers in Cimarron County, Oklahoma, like this one in April 1936, experienced some of the worst conditions in the Dust Bowl. Some had ▽ to raise fences to keep them from being buried by sand.

LIFE IN THE DIRTY THIRTIES

The loose soil caused dust storms large and small in the plains states during the 1930s. In fact people began calling the time "The Dirty Thirties." Huge black clouds would roll in on the horizon without warning. Visibility dropped to zero. Drivers, unable to see the road, were stranded as their engines clogged with dust. School children couldn't find their way home in the blinding storms. *"A severe dust storm raged over the city all day, could not see Dibbles plaza, nor to get around in the house without a light,"* Mabel Holmes, from Topeka, Kansas, wrote in her diary March 20, 1935. *"The houses are in a terrible condition from the storm. Was over an [hour] getting dust off of porches & walks ..."* she recorded the following day.

△ Some people wore old gas masks from World War I (1914–1918) to protect themselves from the dust.

The dry air caused by drought and dust storms caused static electricity to build up. Neighbors stopped shaking hands so they wouldn't shock one another.

People began wearing goggles to keep the sand from hurting their eyes. They wrapped bandanas around their mouths and noses to keep the dust out. Dust polluted food and water. Even worse, the dust caused severe **respiratory** problems. "Dust pneumonia" was common and deadly.

respiratory—related to the process of breathing

FARMS BECOME DESERTS

Year after year brought drought and blowing dust. It took its toll on farmers and ranchers. Caroline Henderson settled in the panhandle of Oklahoma in 1907. She raised turkeys, millet, and wheat. But the land she loved and tended became a barren desert within 30 years. In a letter dated July 26, 1935, she wrote, *"Now we are facing a fourth year of failure. There can be no wheat for us in 1935 in spite of all our careful and expensive work in preparing ground, sowing and resowing our allotted acreage. Native grass pastures are permanently damaged, in many cases hopelessly ruined, smothered under by drifted sand."*

The extreme drought and soil erosion ruined crops. It also ruined farmers. One farmer explained what happened to his money. *"I put mine in what I thought was the best investment—the good old earth—but we lost on that, too. The finance [company] caught up with us, the **mortgage** [company] caught up with us. Managed to lose $12,000 in three years. My boys have no more future than I have, so far as I can see ahead."*

mortgage—a loan from a bank to buy property

▽ Sand drifts taller than cars covered the land near Dalhart, Texas.

DESPERATION

As farmers' crops withered and died, so did their plans for the future. With no wheat to sell, farmers couldn't buy food or clothing. They couldn't pay the loans on their farms or their farm equipment. They couldn't buy seed to plant for next year. On returning to her hometown in Oklahoma in 1934, Sanora Babb wrote, *"The little main street was quiet ... No one came in and out of the stores ... There wasn't any life anywhere. From each end of the main street I could look out onto the [drought]-desolated fields where no new crops were planted or would be planted this spring."*

DUST BLAST
AGAIN SWEEPS
MID-WEST U.S.A.

Last Hopes Of Wheat
Crops Fade

RAIN AND SNOW IN
OTHER REGIONS

Unprecedented Conditions

Special Cables To "The Advertiser"
GARDEN CITY, Kansas, April 10.
Western Kansas farmers today gave up hopes of a wheat crop. A new dust-storm, denser and more destructive than the dozens that have already swept their fields, today tugged at what vegetation remained, and threatened to leave the western third of the State

Headlines like this one from a Kansas newspaper on April 12, 1935, showed how desperate the situation in the Dust Bowl had become.

△ Animals, like these in Muskogee, Oklahoma, in July 1939, grew lean as food supplies emptied. Without money or crops, farmers had no way to refill their supplies.

With no money in their pockets and no harvest to sell, farmers became desperate. Without water to grow grass or feed, their cows, pigs, and sheep starved. Day by day their hungry families came closer to starvation as well.

CITIES IN RUIN

Hardship spread out from farms like dominos toppling one another. Banks and shops couldn't collect on credit given to broke farmers. Store after store closed. Busy downtown areas turned to deserted ghost towns. In Cimarron County, Oklahoma, teachers weren't given paychecks. They received IOUs, promising to pay them later. Money, like the rain, was in short supply.

The Great Depression only added to the money problems. The Depression began with the stock market crash in 1929 and lasted more than 10 years. Banks closed. Businesses went **bankrupt**, and people lost their jobs.

To help the people, President Roosevelt formed the Public Works Administration (PWA) and the Works Progress Administration (WPA) to create jobs.

△ For sale signs, like this one from October 1938 in Jefferson County, Kansas, dotted the land. As people went bankrupt, they were forced to sell their homes.

Between 1935 and 1943, the WPA created more than 8 million jobs, making it the largest U.S. employer during the time of the Dust Bowl.

bankrupt—unable to pay debts

◁ a poster advertising the Works Progress Administration

"... we must put them to work for a decent wage, and when we reach that decision we kill two birds with one stone, because these families will earn enough by working, not only to subsist themselves, but to buy food for their stock, and seed for next year's planting."

—*President Roosevelt*

The PWA and WPA created jobs to drill wells, pave roads, and build bridges. Wayne Lewis, whose father was employed by the WPA, explained, *"... if you were the ones that had the shovel, it was the difference between starving and having food to eat."* But others thought the work done by the WPA was useless and wasted money. They thought many workers got paid to do very little. Some even said WPA stood for "We're Probably Asleep."

CALIFORNIA, HERE WE COME

Drought, dust, and unemployment drove 2.5 million people to move away from the Dust Bowl. For many a trip west on Route 66 was their last hope. The historic highway ran from Chicago, Illinois, to Santa Monica, California. Nearly 10 percent of those fleeing the Dust Bowl headed for California.

The migrants were homeless, penniless, and unemployed. In desperation many traveled 1,200 miles (1,930 km) or more in search of a better life. One traveler said, *"Do you reckon I'd be out on the highway if I had it good at home?"*

△ Taken in April 1935 near Bakersfield, California, photographer Dorothea Lange captured how families loaded up everything they owned and headed west in search of work.

With nowhere else to go, migrants camped on roadsides in California and other states.

But the millions of Dust Bowl migrants often faced **discrimination**. Store owners refused to wait on them. Police tore down their makeshift camps along the roads. In Los Angeles the chief of police claimed, *"... the hordes of indigents [migrants] are not coming to California for work. They are coming to get on relief rolls, to beg and to steal."*

Although only about 20 percent of the Dust Bowl migrants came from Oklahoma, all the migrants were commonly referred to as "Okies."

The Oklahoma panhandle, one of the hardest hit areas of the Dust Bowl, lost 28 percent of its population over 10 years.

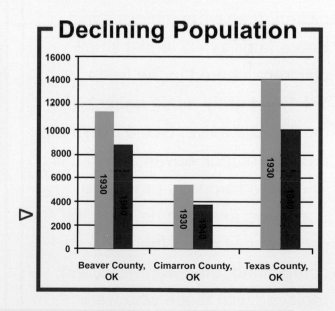

Declining Population

	Beaver County, OK	Cimarron County, OK	Texas County, OK
1930	11400	5400	14000
1940	8700	3700	9900

discrimination—unfair treatment of a person or group, often because of race, gender, or age

A FLOOD OF WORKERS

Employers looking for cheap labor gave handbills to migrants along Route 66. One handbill advertised, *"Cotton Pickers: 5000 Families Wanted."*

Thousands of laborers flooded the West in search of these jobs. But the jobs were few. And they lasted only a short time. Even those able to find work were soon out of luck. Once the crops were picked, they were jobless again. Entire families, including small children, labored in the fields. Yet they barely made enough money to survive. Some dishonest employers took advantage of this. They hired workers promising one wage and then dropped the pay the next day. When workers complained, they were fired and replaced with those who were willing to work for less.

72 • MIGRATORY COTTON PICKERS IN ARIZONA

Cotton Pickers

5000 Families Wanted
240,000 Acres Cotton

IN THE BIG COTTON DISTRICTS—NEAR

PHOENIX	SCOTTSDALE
BUCKEYE	GLENDALE
LITCHFIELD	PEORIA
AVONDALE	MARINETTE
GRIGGS	WADDELL
LAVEEN	QUEEN CREEK
TEMPE	COOLIDGE
MESA	CASA GRANDE
CHANDLER	FLORENCE
GILBERT	ELOY

Big Crop   Heavy Picking
CABINS OR TENTS FREE—GOOD CAMPS
SEVERAL MONTHS' WORK — WARM DRY WINTERS

APPLY AT ANY GIN—OR AT
28 West Jefferson Street
PHOENIX, ARIZONA

Farm Labor Service
CO-OPERATING WITH
UNITED STATES FARM PLACEMENT SERVICE

FIG. 13 - HANDBILL DISTRIBUTED BY THE FARM LABOR
SERVICE, USING THE NAME OF THE
U.S. FARM PLACEMENT SERVICE

AF- 3054, WPA

A migrant worker named Lester Hunter penned a song about the problem in 1938.

"From the east and west and north and south,
Like a swarm of bees we come;
The migratory workers
Are worse off than a bum.
We go to Mr. Farmer
And ask him what he'll pay;
He says, 'You gypsy workers
Can live on a buck a day.'"

Migrant workers in California earned 25 cents an hour pruning, digging ditches, and spraying trees in February 1936.

△ At the end of a long day, migrant workers near Westley, California, in April 1938 waited in line to weigh the peas they picked.

CRITICAL THINKING

Compare Lester Hunter's song lyrics with the advertisement for cotton pickers. What words do the primary sources use to describe the migrant jobs? How do the two sources conflict?

GOVERNMENT CAMPS

Out of work, out of money, and out of hope, many Dust Bowl migrants were worse off than before they headed west. In a newspaper article, author John Steinbeck described these desperate people. *"They arrive in California usually having used up every resource to get here, even to the selling of the poor blankets and utensils and tools on the way to buy gasoline. They arrive bewildered and beaten and usually in a state of semi-starvation, with only one necessity to face immediately, and that is to find work at any wage in order that the family may eat."*

Migrants camped out on roadsides and near farmland. Soon it became clear that the government needed to set up camps. In 1935 California opened its first camp for migrant farmworkers. At the camps families could sleep on wooden slabs and use indoor toilets and showers. First lady Eleanor Roosevelt visited the camps. She said there was a *"dire need"* for them. The first lady added, California *"is doing many commendable things for the migrant workers. There will always be the need for migrant workers but it is my hope that some day many of them will be able to establish a permanent home."*

CRITICAL THINKING

The Migrant Mother photo is one of the most famous images of the Dust Bowl. How does this photograph capture the conditions faced by migrant workers?

▲ Dorothea Lange documented migrants' lives in pictures. Her most famous photograph, "Migrant Mother," shows Florence Owens Thompson and her children in Nipomo, California, in 1936.

A PERMANENT HOME

Camp life was hard, but it was better than life on the road. Still, the Dust Bowl **refugees** longed for homes of their own. Some found the broken dreams of life in California unbearable. After a few years they traveled Route 66 back to where they came from. In a letter to friends one man wrote, *"California is all right for Californians, but we're going back ... A fellow don't appreciate home until he comes to California."*

But many others stuck it out and made new lives for themselves in the West. A California newspaper reported, *"'We ... are being treated just fine,' said Mrs. Jenkins today, beaming at her visitors from her tent at the Shafter migratory camp. Here with 170 other families, the Jenkinses are finding haven while the men folk look for work."* Despite the hardships, many finally found the permanent homes Eleanor Roosevelt spoke of. Sanora Babb, who helped the refugees in the camps, wrote to her sister Dorothy in 1938. *"They are the real descendants of the American pioneers, and if you'd see the spirit in them, you'd never cease to wonder."*

refugee—a person forced to flee his or her home because of natural disaster or war

△ the Shafter migratory camp in June 1938

HEALING THE LAND

The Dust Bowl caused government leaders to think about how land and water were used. President Roosevelt signed the Soil Conservation Act in 1935. The act stated soil erosion *"is a menace to the national welfare ..."* It recognized that soil and water must be protected. The president ordered state governments to make districts to study and prevent soil erosion.

As a result of the act, farmers in the Great Plains were encouraged to grow crops that used less water. They were taught to let some land go unused every few years, letting the soil replenish its nutrients. In addition the government recognized the importance of preserving the grasslands. National grasslands, though less famous than national parks such as Yellowstone, help conserve the Great Plains grass.

As part of the act, landowners had to meet to develop conservation plans.

STARVED
BY LACK OF
PLANT FOOD

NOURISHED
ON
PHOSPHATE
AND LIME

△ After Roosevelt signed the Conservation Act, local soil conservation groups began to test farming techniques. Those tests led to farming operations that are still used today.

The harsh conditions of the Dust Bowl taught people difficult lessons. Everyone began to understand the importance of the very dirt beneath their feet. People learned to respect and care for the land. For in the words of Eleanor Roosevelt, *"Strange to say, conservation of land and conservation of people frequently go hand in hand."*

SELECTED BIBLIOGRAPHY

Babb, Sanora. *On the Dirty Plate Trail: Remembering the Dust Bowl Refugee Camps.* Austin: University of Texas Press, 2007.

Cronin, Francis D., Howard W. Beers, et al. "Works Progress Administration Research Bulletin: Areas of Intense Drought Distress, 1930–1936." Online by Federal Reserve Archive. http://fraser.stlouisfed.org/docs/publications/books/aidd_wpa_1937.pdf

Dayton, Duncan. *The Dust Bowl: An Illustrated History.* San Francisco: Chronicle Books, 2012.

Holmes, Mabel. "Diary Entries" March 15–March 22, 1935–1939. Online by the Kansas Historical Society and Kansas Historical Foundation. http://www.kansasmemory.org/item/210784/text

Hunter, Lester. "I'd Rather Not Be on Relief." 1938. Online by the Library of Congress American Memory. http://memory.loc.gov/afc/afcts/images/st045/0001d.tif

Lange, Dorothea, and Paul Schuster Taylor. *An American Exodus: A Record of Human Erosion.* New York: Reynal & Hitchcock, 1939.

Roosevelt, Franklin D. "Fireside Chat.," September 6, 1936. Online by Gerhard Peters and John T. Woolley, *The American Presidency Project.* http://www.presidency.ucsb.edu/ws/?pid=15122

Roosevelt, Franklin D. "Summary of the Great Plains Drought Area Committee's Preliminary Report and Conclusions Submitted during Drought Inspection Trip.," August 27, 1936. Online by Gerhard Peters and John T. Woolley, *The American Presidency Project.* http://www.presidency.ucsb.edu/ws/?pid=15104

Steinbeck, John. *The Harvest Gypsies: On the Road to the Grapes of Wrath.* Berkeley: Heyday Books, 1988.

GLOSSARY

bankrupt (BAYNK-rupt)—unable to pay debts

depression (di-PRE-shuhn)—a period during which business, jobs, and stock values stay low

discrimination (dis-kri-muh-NAY-shuhn)—unfair treatment of a person or group, often because of race, religion, gender, sexual preference, or age

erosion (i-ROH-zhuhn)—the wearing away of land by water or wind

Great Plains (GRAYT PLAYNS)—the broad, level land that stretches eastward from the base of the Rocky Mountains for about 400 miles (644 km) in the United States and Canada

mortgage (MOR-gij)—a loan from a bank to buy property

nutrient (NOO-tree-uhnt)—a substance needed by a living thing to stay healthy

panhandle (PAN-han-duhl)—a narrow area of land that sticks out from a larger land area; on a map a panhandle looks like the handle of a frying pan

refugee (ref-yuh-JEE)—a person forced to flee his or her home because of natural disaster or war

respiratory (RESS-pi-ruh-taw-ree)—related to the process of breathing

INTERNET SITES

FactHound offers a safe, fun way to find Internet sites related to this book. All of the sites on FactHound have been researched by our staff.

Here's all you do:

Visit *www.facthound.com*

Type in this code: 9781491418406

Check out projects, games and lots more at
www.capstonekids.com

INDEX